Whispers

of the

White Dove

Inspirational Poetry

Pam Sears

ISBN: 978-1540751508

First Printing: January, 2017

Published by 102nd Place LLC
Scottsdale, AZ 85266

Dedication

This book is dedicated to my two sons, Arthur and Douglas who have always been supportive of me and continue to encourage me to follow my dreams.

I also want to thank Mama, who taught me unconditional love and how to be strong.

❧ *Arthur* ❧

Stand proud and tall
Of who you are
Your awesome life
Has come so far
You worked so hard
And made me proud
Your light shines bright
A rainbow in the cloud
Your heart always caring
For others I see
You're becoming the man
I knew you could be
Remember to love
And help others in life
Reach above and beyond
Even at times of strife
With passion and joy
Please choose your path
Live in the heart
And remember to laugh
You bring me joy
I'm so proud of you
So go live your life
Show pride in all you do

Douglas

At first glance at birth
You looked so much like me
To watch you grow up
I anticipated with glee
The hair so blonde
Like shimmering gold
And the dimples to match
What a future to behold
So much like me
Including the smile
Your eyes light up
For you I'd walk ten miles
Your soul full of joy
Your hugs oh so tight
And when someone's been wronged
You put up quite a fight
Your loyalty shows
A friend thru and thru
No matter the struggles
You always stay true
Voicing what you perceive
Your emotions so strong
In this world of woes

You so much belong
I see as you grow
You fight for the cause
You help those in need
Without even a pause
Your light shines so bright
Your soul shines right thru
As you enter adulthood
You'll know what to do
Help others in need
You have so much to share
And such a big heart
It proves that you care
I love you so deep
I'm so proud of you
Sometimes I don't show it
But know this is true

 *Mama*

You loved, you danced
you struggled, you lived
no matter the hardships
You had so much to give

I saw your pain
but you carried on
Your children were cared for
Truly above and beyond

the things you gave up
sacrificed for us all
shows a true mother's love
and you heeded the call

I learned much from you
to be strong and stand tall
to pick myself up
after each and every fall

Your light shines so bright
and will always be there
to show me the way
when it gets hard to bare

I look at the stars
and I see your face
and know that forever
you will be there to embrace

to hold me so tight
to wipe away tears
to share in my joy
and to soothe my fears

I know where you are
and who you are with
and it brings me comfort
what a precious gift

I am so proud of you
for giving me life
and always being there
in my Joy and my strife

I love you so much
you are so very dear
and from this day forward
I know you are near

To love me, to guide me
to watch over us all
to continue to help us
whenever we fall . . .

Thank you Mama :)

Table of Contents

Introduction

I have always felt a strong connection to the White dove and chose to take the name years ago, using it as my online title in spiritual chat rooms. My spiritual group gave me the nickname "Dovey" which is still used today.

One day while in meditation, a vision came to me. I saw a beautiful Native American woman, uniquely adorned, galloping across the open plains on a horse. She stopped and dismounted at a tree where a native brave was leaning. He had an arrow in his shoulder. She removed a medicine pouch from around her waist and began to tend to him.

In my mind I asked "who is this" to which the reply came, "it is you White dove". An elder told me this was a past life and that I had seen it to remind me that I had carried over the healing into this lifetime.

The White dove will forever be my totem animal and spirit guide.

Pam Sears

TOLERANCE

Break Down the Walls

❖❖❖❖❖❖❖

Encased within
as hard as stone
letting no one in
choosing to be alone

It served you well
a long time ago
what built those walls?
Do you even know?

Break down the walls
and let me in
I'll show you a place
where love begins

Where did it begin?
What happened to you?
Who caused such Pain?
what did they do?

I see past those walls
to the love deep inside
I yearn to hold you
so you no longer hide

Break down the walls
and let me in
I'll show you a place
where love begins

Why you so afraid?
to reach out for love
to touch that rainbow
which waits high above

You missin out on life
all the pure joy it brings
to listen to birds
and the songs they sing

Break down the walls
and let me in
I'll show you a place
where love begins

So give me a chance
and please let me in
a journey awaits us

just say when . . .
I make a vow
to go real slow
and let you guide me
so you can let go

Break down the walls
and let me in
I'll show you a place
where love begins . . .

ᴥGood Enough ᴥ

Good enough to live
Good enough to be
Good enough to love
Good enough to see
We are all of that
And so much more
We are good enough For God
To love and adore
Our own unique smile
Our own unique eyes
To say we are pretty
And admit it's not lies
Created to love
Created to be
Created to grow
Created to be free

So what is within

Is also without

The pretty inside

Shines through with a shout

Accept who we are

Please let it shine

We are all so truly

A spark of the Divine

Good enough to laugh

Good enough to cry

Good enough to be loved

And to sing, dance and fly!

❧ *Endure* ❧

Face the pain

Accept the strife

Don't fight the cause

It's part of life

Let it flow

Allow it to be

To face it head-on

Allows us to see

that through the struggle

By climbing uphill

Choosing to fight

It's part of free will

Our choice to accept

Or fight tooth and nail

To accept it as growth

Or to put us in jail

To imprison the soul

Not allowing the tests

Keeps it forever chained

But the soul never rests

It longs to be free

To learn and to grow

And once it's allowed

Makes life go with the flow

Accept and endure

And after you'll see

By walking the path

Those tests set your free

The path is so long

So lighten the load

Releasing that baggage

Helps in walking that road

It quickens our steps

With less to carry

Makes the journey smoother

And so much less harried

Of course it is tough

And at times hard to bare

But with each lesson learned

Makes us much more aware

In helping ourselves

Gives us wisdom to share

Helps us reach out to others

Letting them know we care

It's part of the plan

To reach out in love

So endure all those tests

And watch smiles from above . . .

Smile

It's so simple really

God's bigger plan

Trust in the path

Smile all you can

The journey's the fun

Just let things be

Walk the yellow brick road

At the end you will see

Reach out with love

Be filled with pure joy

To play on this Earth

That's our real "Toy"

You know what you know

Deep down inside

Always follow the heart

And enjoy the whole ride

Smile when it gets rough

Smile when you are sad

Smile when you get angry

Life's not really so bad

Conquer those fears

And those ruts in the road

By giving them a smile

Helps to ease your load

Reach out to those hurting

Just give them a smile

Throw in a huge hug

And sit with them awhile

It's part of God's plan

So simple you see

It's all about LOVE

So smile and be free . . .

Strength of a Rock

❖❖❖❖❖❖❖

Skipped across water

Ripples cascading about

Waves go on forever

The affect shows no doubt

Of strength to endure

Full echoes abound

Creating fluid motion

And a so serene sound

All covering the earth

Staying strong although weathered

It's grounded to Earth

It is home and stays tethered

Thru storms and rain

And blistering winds

Each day it's still there

Showing its strength yet again

It firmly remains

And forever lives

Its beauty beholding

It knows what it is

I shall be this rock

So strong and sure

Enduring the path

Even when it's obscure

This rock and I

We are kindred souls

We both choose to endure

Life's ebbs and flows . . .

The Path

*T*he path abounds
as I look around
to see the way
of a bright new day

To live... to love
to touch the sky
and on my knees
I begin to cry

A heart so filled
so full of Joy
tis like a child
with a brand new toy

Each day is to learn
and teach and to share
and reach out to others
if only we dare

I reach out to you
with a story to share
you open your heart
and listen with care

You reach out to me
the circle complete
each one learning something
to hold to so sweet

Our paths have then crossed
if for only awhile
and that spirit connection
brings with it a smile . . .

Worthy of Love

When one cannot love

From deep within the heart

It causes much pain

Keeping intimacy apart

But that does not mean

You aren't worthy of love

It's set into motion

From very high above

To be unable to love

Is sadness within

Causes life to stop

Rather than begin

Do not let their pain

Cause a lacking in you

When true reality is

You are love thru and thru

Another can't take

Our own love away

We still have it to give

To send forth each day

You are so loved

So worthy to receive

For in essence you are love

Although at times hard to perceive

The true beauty of love

Allows you to see

That by sending them love

Just might set them free

By sending them love

Although they can't in return

Might give them a spark

Lest their soul perhaps yearn

They might find this love

Deep inside of them

And so with each sunrise

Send it forth yet again

But remember the truth

You are worthy of love

Worthy to receive

Worthy to be hugged

You ARE love . . .

INSPIRATION

Flying

To take on wings
to catch the breeze
to soar with the rainbow
and do so with ease

To be so free
is this not bliss?
to reach every star
not a one being missed

To feel the air
to reach the sun
to find that place
where life has begun

Once you learn to fly
no limits abound
freedom sets in
there's love all around

To be able to fly
takes letting go
of what holds you back
the old stuff, ya know?

But when you do
and you take that flight
the wonder of it all
brings with it the light

The freedom, the love
the joy of your wings
joining with all creation
what pure joy that brings

Take flight with me now?
No telling what we will find
an adventure awaits us
once we leave "old stuff" behind

There's new things to find
to reach out and see
to replace the old
and set our hearts free . . .

Delight in Flight

Taking the flight

Beyond the veil

Eyes fully opened

A true story it tells

Seeing through the mist

To a world beyond

Of hopes and dreams

Creating a bond

The sparkle, the light

The magic of it all

My heart swells with Love

And I heed the call

The journey of life

Entails much more you see

Than just sitting on Earth

To do more than just be

As if to have wings

To soar past the sky

And seeing much more

Than just the mind's eye

Not only to see

But to feel and to touch

Aww, the wonder of magic

Makes me ponder much

And while I ponder

I soar in glee

Chasing the rainbow

And it sets me free

The delight in flight

Brings with it a smile

And I sit on a cloud

Being as One for a while . . .

The Fire Within

*I*t came as a bolt
of lightning so strong

it awakened my heart

and put there a song

It burns ever so bright

and lights up the way

it shows me adventure

in the dawn of each day

The passion so strong

the need so clear

my vision now shown

of what to hold dear

The heart now so opened

the love burns so deep

and I shall never let go

this love I will keep

Not only to keep

but to give and to share

the heat of this fire

makes me much more aware

That I am a rainbow

and the sunset each night

and part of the sun

each day burning bright

I am a gentle stream

a clear waterfall

I am part of the tree

that stands proud and tall

I am a hawk soaring high

a horse running free

an eagle with sight

and an otter with glee

This fire within

brings passions so strong

I cry out in Joy

and know I belong . . .

⮹ *Illusions* ⮹

Look upon your path

What do you see?

Is it truly there?

Is it reality?

If you look beyond

Glance left or right

Those goals you have set

Are they truly in sight?

Or is what you see

Clouded with fear

For to see it right

You must persevere

Do you truly see

Beyond the veil?

What's in the mirror?

To let you set sail

For in order to see

Your path so clear

You must let it go

The illusions, the fear

For what you see

With the Mind's eye view

Does not truly match

What your heart always knew

Life is not what it seems

The path not so clear

For all that we thought

And held to so dear

Let go of the fog

Let it clear away

Just look with the heart

And see a different day

Don't look with the mind

Don't look with the eye

Search from within the heart

There your answers lie

There are other senses

Such as touch, taste and feel

Tap into those closely

Then you can see what is real

What will you find then?

Oh what a surprise!

The Higher Self

Is so kind and wise

We are all an illusion

On this planet Earth

Stumbling and falling

Awaiting true birth

So continue to search

But with heart not eyes

So much we have seen

Are all truly lies

We are more than we think

More than we see

We are mysterious creatures

Who long to be free . . .

Do You Know?

❖❖❖❖❖❖

Do you know the smile of a child?

Watch the sunshine and glee

The pure joy of life

To be flying and free?

Do you know the stars

That glisten each night?

Taking time to watch them

So shimmering and bright?

Do you know a sunset

At the end of each day?

To sit, ponder and wonder

Watching it drift away?

Do you know of the kitten

Without hardly a care?

She nuzzles your neck

Such love does she share

Do you know of a song

That touches your soul?

That makes you sing

And thus makes you glow?

Do you know of a mountain

To sit and be still?

To listen to nature

Bringing with it a thrill?

Do you know of a bird

Watch it soar in the sky?

And imagine yourself

Flying with it so high?

Do you know of a place

Only you can see?

Created just for you

Your sanctuary?

Do you know you are loved

And never alone?

Sit still and be quiet

And you will be shown

Do you know who you are

A sparkle of light?

That God tucks in

Each and every night

Do you know where you'll be

At the end of this path?

That same sparkle of light

And thus you will laugh

Do you know when you smile

It comes back to you

The same with a hug

It sticks like glue

Do you know we are one?

We're related you see

All came from one Source

Including the tree

Do you know who I am?

I am part of you

Look into my heart

You'll know this is true

Smile of a Dove

This day of days

just sit and smile

knowing another

will hold you awhile

feel the warmth

the love within

aww . . . sense the magic

as the new day begins

know you are loved

from the depths of the soul

a smile touches my face

and the heart stays aglow

remember the gifts

you receive each day

and find the magic

it helps show you the way

if things get too rough

see the smile of a dove

and know you are cared for

from high up above . . .

New Journey

Take me up high

Soaring with wings

To a brand new place

Where my soul can still sing

A place of Love

Helping and healing

Walking the path

Along the way seeing

The path always changes

The soul knows where to go

When it yearns to seek knowledge

And thus continue to grow

Life brings with it changes

Sometimes filled with pain

But it longs to be free

Returning home once again

Although home is within

And always will be

The path takes it turns

Giving new places to see

New souls to encounter

Connections to be made

Like sharing a tree

When both seek the shade

The excitement of Life

Such wonders to behold

I await the new journey

It shimmers of gold . . .

FAITH

✎ *Believe* ✎

Believe it is real

You are never apart

See it thru the eyes

Feel it in the heart

Believe it is there

Imagine the cord

It holds you connected

Strong as a board

Have faith in the love

Reach out in the dark

A hand awaits you

Causing a spark

This spark does shine

A tapestry it weaves

It comes in the dawn

When you simply believe . . .

Circle of Doors

The corridor is long

From beginning to end

And along the way

Are choices within

Each door holds a place

And idea, a thought

Of which way to turn

Take this one or not?

No matter which door

One decides to choose

All have a place

With nothing to lose

In choosing one door

The path then unfolds

And then there will come

Another door to behold

And so it's a circle

Each door will be met

At the appointed time

Perhaps all preset

So worry not

Which choices you make

For all will be opened

And none will you forsake

Let go of fear

Let go of doubt

Embrace each choice

With a smile and a shout

For at least you have chosen

And moved forward you see

You didn't stand still

And that sets you free

The Journey

Come out of the darkness

and see the light

let fears go on by

and get back the sight

Look beyond to the sun

and see what's ahead

no need to look back

the past is now shed

There is only today

tomorrow will come

based on actions we do

new paths have begun

Enjoy all the journey

life's an adventure you see

So enjoy each day

and always be free

To reach out and love all

to touch even one soul

to help one another

Is this not our goal?

Like skipping a stone

across clear water you see

starts a ripple affect

and sets more souls free . . .

Dragonfly Sings

Dragonfly sings her song

in a world where illusion doesn't belong

she flies with the wind where her song can
be heard

it carries her voice, word for word

the melody lures, it bursts as the sun

taking us back before life had begun

to another world, another place

a life prior to the human race

she sings her song to remind us all

look past the illusions, break down the wall

she sings of truth in her power of flight

and from her wings, shines forth pure light

when you see her approach, sit still and
hear

the words could be saying 'change is near'

her song is of power, truth and light

trust in her words, and you shall take flight

Go with the Flow

❧•❧•❧•❧•❧•❧

You think life is a struggle
and so hard to bare
remember who you are
and stay aware

You're a miracle to behold
a spark of the Divine
let in the light
and you shall surely shine

As lessons creep in
sometimes, two, three or four
don't fight the feelings
let open the door
Your soul wants to grow
to experience and learn
so grab hold onto faith
and let the heart yearn

We long for home
that unconditional love
and know we can reach it
way high up above

Yet we can find it here
as we reach for another
to look in their eyes
we can all be Mothers
We set up our paths
to come here and see
can we find Heaven on Earth?
Yes! . . . and always be free

So give a big smile
each day to the Sun
and know in your life
an adventure's begun

Magical Journey

❖❖❖❖❖❖❖

To awaken each day

See the sunlight begin

To feel total love

Brings on a huge grin

What awaits me this day?

I can't wait to see

It's always so magical

And I dance 'round with glee

Will it be a rainbow?

Oh, please make it three

And so when they come

Reminds me I'm free

I ask for the magic

Each day when I rise

And I know it will come

And it's always a surprise!

I ask and I get

What more can I say?

To find wonder and magic

Each and every day

My heart soars so high

My love only grows

And I'm so very thankful

For what Creator has bestowed

I take what comes

And attempt to share

My magical journey

And cry out with a flare!

I take this magic

Place it gently without

And share it with others

It's what my journey's about

In sharing the magic

And sending out love

Joins our souls closer

To Creator above

Come share in the magic

And I'll give you a smile

I'll put arms around you

Letting cares go for awhile

I offer my love

Can you hear the call?

Can you feel your own magic?

Finding Oneness with all?

Oh yes it is there

For all to see

Go seek out the magic

And you'll dance 'round with glee . . .

 *When?*

When will it come?

How long must I wait?

Will it come this lifetime?

And what is my fate?

To wonder each day

To ask and not hear

Yet stay on the path

Working past the fear

Taking each day

Not knowing for sure

Yet finding the magic

Brings with it the lure

Continue to seek

Find magic each day

Look for the rainbow

It will show you the way

In time answers come

And the way becomes clear

You will look back and ask

So what was that fear?

But of course you do know

The answer is within

Hear the words come

They float on the wind

The timing is right

It's always so

Trust what you feel

And bask in the glow

HEALING

And So It Is . . .

Stepping back from life

Aww, if only I could

To stay in that place

Where all is so Good

But alas I chose

This form, this shell

Allowing the tests

Where the lessons dwell

A chance to learn

A chance to grow

And helping to heal

Souls I meet and know

Remembering me

What I chose to do

Helps in those times

When I'm feeling so blue

Yes pain comes at times

It cuts so deep

But thru it all

The Love I shall keep

I love and love

Even thru the tears

It's brought me this far

Thru all the years . . .

A Child

A child is lonely

And scared in the night

A hand reaches out

Caressing the child in light

Holding and hugging

And sending pure love

With much aided help

From angels above

Heart touches heart

Soul touches soul

Smile touches smile

Unconditional love is the goal

A child has this love

Look into the eyes and see

A child touches the heart

And so sets it free

A gift from God

To show us the way

It's all about love

Each and every day

So watch a child smile

See the sparkle within

As they chase after bubbles

With one huge grin

A child knows the secret

Hidden within that smile

If you wish to know it

Just sit with them awhile

The answer is there

For all to see

Their love will astound you

And set your soul free

Dragonfly Speaks

rayers go out

Cries to the wind

Seeking solace

Asking pain to rescind

Dragonfly comes

Flying into my face

"Listen to the wind"

He says with such grace

He flutters about

I shoo him away

Only to have him return

The very next day

He dances before me

And repeats his song

"Listen to the wind"

"It will help you along"

I cannot hear

Thru all my tears

Can't face the wind

Too many fears

"Listen" he says

And so I try

Feeling the wind

As it floats on by

It will take time

To hear so clear

To see the illusion

And to face the fear

I am strong

Mama taught me to be

So I join with the wind

Watching it carry me

Off to the void

To the place of One

I keep open my Heart

And allow love to come

Fighting the River

She ebbs and flows

merging with the waves

swaying to and fro

cast about at times roughly

it cuts into the soul

She finds a bit of a break ahead

a calmness to the river

allowing her to rest

to catch her breath

where is it going

where is it taking her

she knows not

only to hang on

try to go with the flow

instead of fighting

the fighting brings more angst

more frustrations

more anger

when she surrenders

joins with the water

merging into one

the calmness comes

a brief moment of knowing

knowing all is well

her path written long ago

the fighting is futile

merge, merge

She joins with the water

lets it fill her every being

no longer fighting the river

until the next rapids come

and they will come

She will brace herself again

with each rapid she gains strength

riding the current

until the calmness comes again

She closes her eyes

looks inside her heart

cries her tears

joins with the water

lets go of her fears

❧ *Let Me* ❧

*L*et me learn

Let me grow

Let me live

And forever know

The truth of Love

So deep within

Like a moonlight glow

Of an ocean swim

Let me reach out to you

To hold and to feel

The love within

In Oneness to seal

Let me heal your pain

Replace it with Joy

Filling up the hole

Where once was a void

Let me lean on you

And learn to receive

For that is true love

Allowing you to perceive

Letting you see inside

My love in my heart

Will show you indeed

We are never apart

Let me give you a rainbow

A smile and a hug

Letting go of those cares

With just one lil shrug

Let me show you the magic

That's always there

Just open your eyes

And become more aware

Let me be inside you

As you are inside me

Let's soar up to the rainbow

And together fly free

Let me give you a smile

And caress you with love

Let me shower you with sparkles

Sharing the light from above

Tears of a Dove

She cries into her pillow

Feeling very much in despair

Hurt done to a child

And anger everywhere

The pain in the heart

Yet continuing to love

When dark days come

Golden light shines from above

The words still come

Follow your path

It will become clear

They will feel their wrath

Continue to love

Don't shut them all out

Keep sending healing

Using a smile and a shout

Yes, call it out loud

Those who need you shall hear

Some wish to find healing

And to move past the fear

The tears of a Dove

Are healing they say

So let them flow

Even if every day

Don't give up hope

There is Love around

And caring hearts

That hold the sounds

Of joining hands

With others who see

That there is still hope

Still chances to be free

The tears of a Dove

Feel the hurt and the pain

Echoes in her wings

And she cries out in vain

But her wings then enclose

And caress with love

She's a warrior of light

Pushing the dark back with a shove

The tears of a Dove

Sometimes also brings smiles

Watching rainbows galore

Following clouds for miles

The tears of a Dove

Takes her high up in flight

Soaring with eagles

Touching stars that shine bright

The tears of a Dove

Are also filled with hope

Sharing her love

Helping others to cope

She falls down on her path

Showing bruised and skinned knees

And asking for aid

A bandage please?

She can't see what's ahead

Yet continues on

Knowing that the lesson

Is now truly gone

The tears of a Dove

Cries a few more tears

Then takes the next step

In spite of her fears

A dance and a smile

Seeking magical days

And sharing the love

In such magical ways

The Night Comes

❧❧❧❧❧❧

The night comes
Another day ends

Sadness falls away

My sanctuary begins

It surrounds me strong

Protects me from pain

Reminds me the lessons

Are not all in vain

The journey is tough

But then so am I

Mama raised me thus so

And so I cry

The tears are my strength

My will to survive

I'm more than I think

And I continue to thrive

Bring it on I say

I shall not give in

Nor walk away from it all

Oh yes I shall win

One day I will know

What my life was about

And the growth of the soul

I shall voice with a shout

I trust and have faith

Even thru my tears

That the soul has been growing

Throughout all these years

The heart beats in union

Along with the soul

The light flows thru me

And brings with it a glow

But along with the tears

The pain and hard times

Such love comes to me

Like the sun, it does shine

I'm filled with strength

Hope and desire

And so with my wings

I soar even higher

So truly blessed

Honored and free

My goal shall remain

Be the best I can be . . .

REFLECTION

 *Within*

As life goes on

All around us we see

Rainbows to show us

To sit and just be

To listen to quiet

And go deep inside

You know the place well

Where nothing can hide

For going within

Although hard it may be

Will only enrich us

And set out hearts free

Learning to love

Starts right in that place

The same for us all

No matter what race

For once we do that

And love who we are

We love all others

And connect from afar. . .

Arrival of a Dream

Elusive you were

Beyond my reach

Over the rainbow

Not yet unleashed

You played with me

Taunted and teased

I did not feel

So very pleased

A dangling carrot

Placed before me

Reaching to touch

I saw you flee

Pursuing more

Hungering to own

This elusive secret

For me alone

No one could help

Bring you to me

The choice was mine

Be slave or free

Stopping the chase

Sitting still to think

It came to me

With a brilliant wink

A part of me now

Caressing within

Touching the soul

New life begins

Give me your name

I ask so clear

"I'm Inner Peace"

"You've found me my dear!"

Sedona Journey

❖❖❖❖❖❖❖❖

Among the water

Looking all around

Feeling the joy

And the lovely sound

Feeling the breeze

Seeing purple hues

Connects me closer to God

And brings me clues

I know who I am

And why I am here

The rainbows have shown me

It's now much more clear

I found strength at Boynton

And peace at Oak Creek

The visions remind me

Pure love I still seek

Bell Rock brought me balance

A longing to be free

Even clouds in the sky

Brought a message to me

The healing that came

From Montezuma's Well

Took my pain from me

It's clear as a bell

My Sedona Journey

Brought me peace within

Recharged my soul

Allowing a new journey to begin

∞ *Awakening* ∞

*a*wakening to the Spirit within me, around me

to see God within my eyes

when I glance into a mirror

ah . . . the tears, the Joy

I am so loved . . .

and in this love I reach out to share

to love as One, to be loved as One

how exquisite . . .

to be taken to the place

where I already know who I am

my TRUE self!

and see the illusions, and there are many

to experience this joy

this knowing, of what I am to do

while having this earthly experience

the journey continues for us all

yet our journeys lead to the same
destination

to return home . . .

and I yearn to return home . . .

knowing our purpose fulfilled

our hands and hears touched others

and shared our sparkle

of the Oneness with Creator

we are all truly blessed

and I start each day

in thanks and a smile :)

a knowing within . . .

Touch of the Wind

The gentle caress

the freedom you bring

causes me to smile . . .

to fly, ah . . . to sing

All cares blow on by

and there's nothing to fear

envelope me now

and hold me so dear

My wings catch your breeze

and I soar up so high

to join with the clouds

brings tears to my eyes

To always fly free

no matter what cares

to capture a feeling

to bring back and share

Although I'm alone

just me and my wings

tis an honor to fly

oh what ecstasy it brings

To stay in that moment

and hear whispers of love

and never return

but to stay up above

but alas there is life

and I have to return

yet keeping that essence

of what the heart so yearns

To fly, to soar

to always be free

to sit in the clouds

just being with me . . .

Reflections

Days gone by

anything missed?

forgotten?

ignored?

Weeks gone by

anyone missed?

forgotten?

ignored?

Did we reach out

to the lonely, the hurting, the angry

What of our own fears?

Did we go inside

to ask why?

Did we let it go?

Any missed opportunities

to learn?

to seek?

to grow?

to Love?

What of the speed bumps?

Did we take them slow?

or did we speed up

to get past them quicker?

What of our paths?

missed any steps

in our learning?

If so, can we go back?

or just forward

trying, yet again?

To grasp our purpose

to live in the now

to walk in the light

and connect as one

To be who we are

accept all that is

no regrets, no guilt

If mistakes were made

did we learn our lessons?

and move another step forward

to reach our goal

ever onward into the light

To walk in the light

to share in the light

to learn in the light

to teach in the light

to connect in the light

to always stay in the light . . .

This I choose now and forever . . .

Sounds of Trains

Sounds of trains

Just like the rains

Soothes the soul

Brings a glow

I do not know

Why I love it so

Each night I hear

The sound so near

Memories past

A thought is caste

Lulls me to dream

Sight unseen

Why does this sound

Bring peace around

Taking me places

Seeing faces

At times I hear

Them both so clear

Rains and trains

Memory remains

Those two sounds

Engulfs, surrounds

Brings such peace

And with it release

Whispers

Alone in the quiet

Whispers come on the wind

Ever so faint and I strain to hear

Voices outreaching

Sending love to the soul

So many voices

I wonder why

Perhaps because I have asked

Seeking to know, to understand

Crying out at times

With angst and despair

The whispers quiet my soul

Embracing with love

One big universal hug

I long to reach them

So far away

But no need to do so

They are a kiss away

A stone's throw in the water

A leaf flying on by

A bird soaring with glee

A child giggling at play

The voices are ever so close

Answers seem to come

If I stay in the quiet

Opening heart and soul

About the Author

❖❖❖❖❖❖❖❖

Pam Sears has been a Licensed Massage Therapist and Bodyworker for over 20 years. She is also an Infant Massage Instructor and Psychic Medium. She worked in the corporate world for 20 years and at age 40 decided to follow her heart and enter into the healing field where she could share her passion and love for helping others. She has a private practice in Peoria, Arizona where she lives with her beloved boxer pit rescue Chelsea.

For more information please visit her website:

www.PamSears.com

or contact her at:

Pam@PamSears.com